A Matter of When

Written and illustrated by Alex C. Potocki

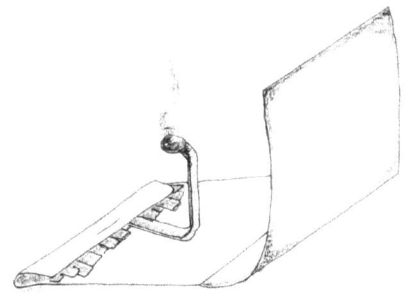

Copyright © 2010 by Alex C. Potocki

WHOAUP

WhoaUp Publishing
1326 N. Main St., Davenport, IA 52803

All rights reserved, including the right to reproduce this book, or portions thereof, in any form.

ISBN 978-0-9845883-0-5

This book is dedicated to everyone that ever was, is and will be.

I can honestly say, without a doubt,
As sure as you are sitting there reading this now,
That aside from amazing,
Life is a maze,
With a single way in, and several ways out.

There once was a boy named Keats,

Who ate a great deal of sweets.

Yet when a strange man

Offered his hand,

Who knew they were the last he would eat.

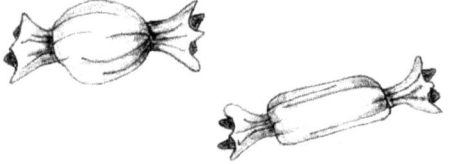

Remember little Toby and his two twin brothers,
The envy of all the neighborhood mothers?
On a flight from Spain,
In the driving rain,
They fell from the sky with two hundred others.

For James, the Army, a family tradition,
And there he was on a top-secret mission.
Sadly in War,
As in Life, you'll agree,
Being killed in action is a lasting condition.

Bobby Lee was bright and full of glee,
Bringing a smile to everyone she'd see.
But I'm sorry to report
That her life was cut short
From one little bee and a dangerous allergy.

There was a boy I knew named Kane,
Who was undoubtedly quite insane.
"Stronger than a locomotive,"
He fervently noted,
But was proved wrong by the No. 6 train.

It was a shame to hear that Shelley had died.

"Such a sweet girl," everyone cried.

But every single day,

People go, people stay.

Shelley chose her way, carbon monoxide.

Susan, we will surely miss you.

From what I hear, there was little they could do.

You slipped and fell,

Hit your head, and, well...

Over the cliff you flew.

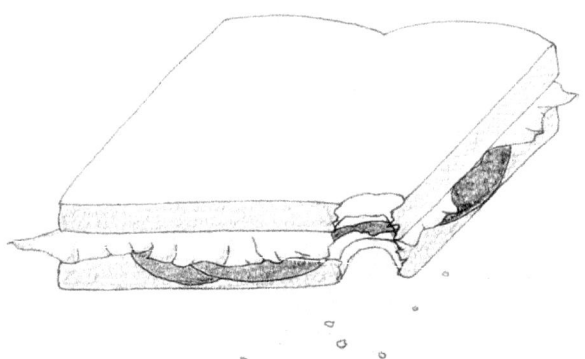

Agnes was truly the best of the bunch.

We can expect great things was everyone's hunch.

So there's a definite lack,

As she's not coming back

From the tasty ham sandwich that she choked on at lunch.

There once was a girl named Betty,
Who lived to the ripe age of seventy.
She outlasted most,
But now she's a ghost.
They found her last June, asleep permanently.

Jack was nimble, as I do recall,
But, in fact, I didn't know him well at all.
He lost his job, his wife,
All his money and his mind,
And taunted the police who ended his fall.

Carlos always had a great sense of humor.
When we first heard, we thought it a rumor.
It's surely a fluke.
There's no way that's true!
Sadly it was, an inoperable tumor.

There once was a girl named Kim,
Who we all thought was horribly thin.
She constantly ate,
But gained no weight.
As she tossed her last cookies, her heart gave in.

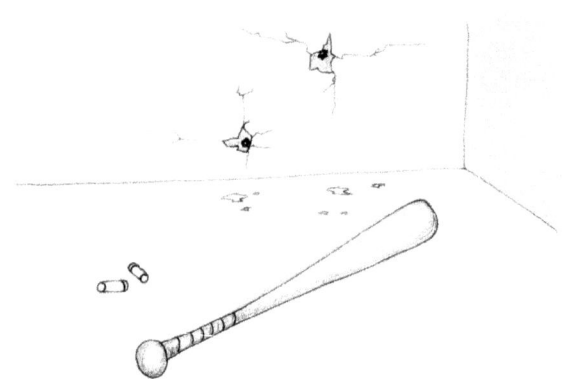

10

Poor, poor, angry Pat,

Always made fun of and always laughed at.

He taught us a lesson,

I'll give you that -

When off to a gunfight, don't take a bat!

There once was a girl named Claire,

A straight-laced type with wavy brown hair.

But after they found

Parts of her husbands in town,

The jury said prison, but the judge said chair.

Gloria we really did adore,

But to her, life was simply a bore.

Waking up anymore

Was a horrible chore.

How many sleeping pills? Three hundred and four.

There once was a girl named Lindsey

Whose health had always been flimsy.

So it was no surprise,

In the middle of July,

When she caught pneumonia and died.

There once was a boy named Stan,
Who dreamed of becoming just like his old man.
But the infection spread quick,
Making him mortally sick,
And laid waste to both him and his plans.

Carrie was independent and full of drive,
The kind of girl who in this world would thrive.
But her directions through the forest
Were obviously the poorest,
As she never made it out alive.

Remember the sister of poor old Claire,

Who approached everything with caution and care?

Looking to the sky,

She was caught by surprise,

And never got up from her trip down the stairs.

There was a young boy named Travis,
Who had a strange and dangerous habit.
You think raging current
Would be a deterrent,
But the lights went dim as he stabbed it.

I once knew a girl named Hope,

Who never smiled, she moped.

And there one day,

Early in May,

She swayed from a very short rope.

I'll never forget the boy named Jay.
Everything seemed to be going his way.
Yet all at once,
On a bright sunny day,
His family, then himself, he willfully did slay.

Let us pause to remember hardworking Ned,
Toiling at the mill until his fingers bled.
It was just bizarre,
The accident, it is said.
He lost three toes, a hand and his head.

There once was a boy named Chuck,

Who always seemed to have the best of luck.

But it must have run out

Playing ball one day,

As he ran in the way of a 10-ton truck.

Kristin, we never did believe her,

But now all we do is grieve for her.

She complained of some pain,

Ah, she's lying again,

But it turned out to be hemorrhagic fever.

I once knew a boy named Cole,

The life of the party he always stole.

But when passing someone slow

On a dark foggy road,

Well, when counting the bodies, he was among the toll.

There once was a boy named Clark,

Who always snuck out after dark.

When he never returned,

We later learned

That most of him was found in the park.

George had it made, a life without strife,
Three kids, a nice job and a loving wife.
But he bumped the wrong man
On his rush to the can,
And wound up stuck with a long, sharp knife.

Remember that neighbor boy we all called Fred?
Words can't describe the kind of life he led.
But one rainy night,
A drunk ran a light.
Now we all sigh, "I can't believe he's dead."

Oh, Tom, we knew you well,

You were harmless, as far as we could tell.

But as Fate would have it,

You'd had had it,

And blew yourself up crying, "See you in Hell."

Pete, ah Pete, he was always so neat,

Fashionable, likable, agreeable and sweet.

But how many times

Do I need to repeat,

Look both ways before crossing the street.

I once knew a boy named Dave,
And exploring new places he craved.
Until one day,
I think a Wednesday,
An unstable cave became his grave.

I remember that girl named Helen,
What she was thinking, there is no telling.
Yet, word on the street,
The wrong guy she did meet,
And she died in prison a felon.

Elanor, Elanor, life without Elanor,

They found her all broken outside the front door.

They can only guess

That to make such a mess,

She must have jumped from the fifty-first floor.

I once knew a boy named Ricktor,

Who thought he was a clever trickster.

'I never lose,'

He'd proudly effuse,

But if Life is a game, Death is always the victor.

I once knew a boy named Trevor,
Who seemed exceedingly clever,
But juggling sharp axes
Without any practice...
Well, that's just the stupidest thing ever.

33

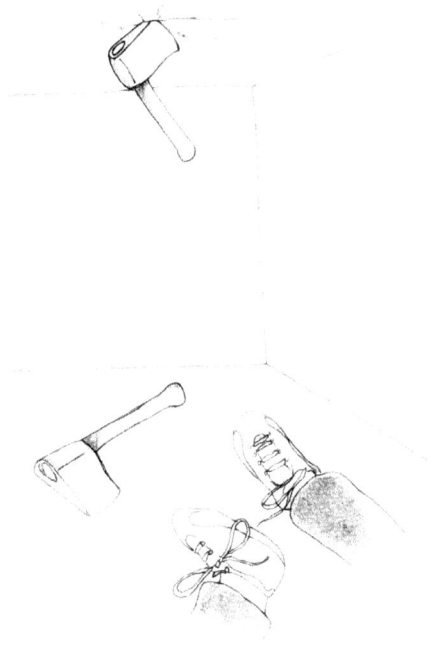

I once knew a girl named Jill,

Who had a craving for pills.

The more she was dealt,

The better she felt,

Until she was found morbidly still.

Gretchen, the cute Southern belle,

Had everyone under her spell.

She would go far,

We could always tell,

If it weren't for her stumble into that deep, forgotten well.

He could never cope with the death of his sister.
In fact, Daniel became increasingly bitter.
He blamed his Dad, his friends
And even the sitter,
Until a loaded revolver made him Life's latest quitter.

Jared was a boy that never gave in,
But if lose he must, it was done with a grin.
"There's always next time,"
He humbly chimed,
As he died from a virus with a taste for skin.

Gregory was a swift boy, he sure ran a lot.

He was the fastest in our class. I kid you not.

But the flesh can't out pace

Death's grim embrace.

He was felled after school by a tiny brain clot.

I once knew a boy named Sammy,

Who went under as they laughed, "He can't swim, can he?"

Well, the answer, I'm afraid,

Surfaced eight days later

All bloated, breathless and clammy.

Remember that smart boy, every test he'd pass,
But he always complained that nice guys finish last?
Well, what do you know,
He got something wrong.
He's already dead, the first of our class.

There once was a boy named Ted
Whose habit was to wish that he was dead.
So with one little slash,
His life drained from the gash,
Turning the bath a dark, eerie red.

There once was a boy named Mike,

The kind of boy you would instantly like.

But meeting him I must mention

Is simply out of the question,

Since he was struck down by a bus while riding his bike.

Christy always dreamed of being a dancer,

But instead, at eleven ,was diagnosed with cancer.

Her parents bemoaned, to the doctor,

"Why her?"

"How long?" they groaned. "Six months" was the answer.

There was a young lad named Chad,
Who linked to tinker a lot.
But when he mixed gas
With his Dad's last match,
Well, his parents now tend to his plot.

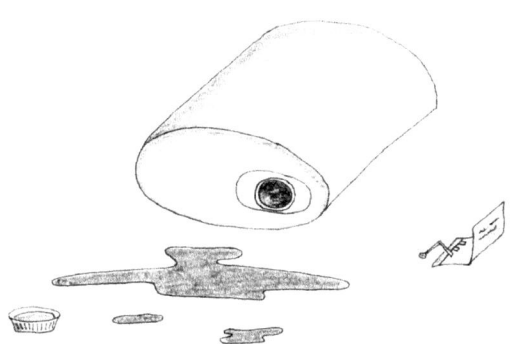

I once knew a girl named Kate,

Who always drank and stayed out late.

But when offered a ride

By that cute guy Clyde,

Well, she was found in six different States.

You've finished the book, let me recommend,

That you take a deep breath, maybe call a good friend.

For you've made it this far,

In Life, that is,

Without meeting some horribly grisly, untimely end.

www.ingramcontent.com/pod-product-compliance
Ingram Content Group UK Ltd.
Pitfield, Milton Keynes, MK11 3LW, UK
UKHW022208230426
12048UKWH00016BA/723